ZINGING SUCCESS COMFORTING FAILURE

PART 2

Published by
Free Spirit

Poets Choice & Free Spirit LLC
First Edition September 2023

Special Thanks To Hardev Matharoo, Toni Kochensparger,
Suzette Blom
Winner of Contest: Sameer Farooqi

Cover Design by Koni Deraz, Germany
Back Cover Content by Akshay Sonthalia, India
Edited by Kaneez Zehra Razavi, India
Book Design by Adil Ilyas, Pakistan
Authors in this book are from -

USA   Canada   France

ISBN: 978-81-19351-39-8
Price: $25
BCID: 618-16997243

Contents

Jayna Locke

Minnetonka, Minnesota - United States

Jayna Locke is a Minnesota writer. She is reachable through her website.

1. Lost Charm

The tiny charm seemed inconsequential. There it sat, lost and abandoned in a puddle that glistened with motor oil. Perhaps it meant something to someone. Perhaps not. For Danielle it fell into the category of treasure, which was how she thought of objects and trinkets she found along roadsides on her well-worn path to her high school.

She picked it up, cleaned its surface with a tissue and put it in her pocket. There was nothing else to do.

At school, something was off. She could sense it the moment she stepped onto the school grounds. An abject fear settled in her stomach. She had a feeling for these things. It happened the day Sonia Parker and her friends surrounded her in the gym locker room and made her touch herself before they would allow her to get dressed. She had known. She had sensed this incident coming—the way birds will sense an oncoming storm— well before the moment she entered the hazing area of the gym locker room.

She had resigned herself to the humiliation then. The burning eyes on her were like red hot fireplace pokers, each piercing a hole in her that felt hot, permanent and cruel. Yet the foreboding sense she'd had that a horrible, sickening incident was coming somehow helped her to endure it when it actually did. She couldn't explain the phenomenon. It just was.

Now she walked through the morning chaos of backpacks, coffee breath and jostling, and looked around. Her best friend, Carly, was nowhere to be seen. They normally found one another near the drinking fountain before first period, but when she trolled past, she only found that people stepped aside for her, as if she took some sort of precedence. One boy that she remembered from science class with a mop of red hair and desultory green eyes even swept his hand out toward the fountain in an "after you" gesture.

She smiled uncomfortably and moved on. Where was Carly? Walking alone through Whimden High was like stepping into a pit of vipers. It was only navigable with a friend by your side. Otherwise unspeakable things could happen. Especially for one in her social standing, which was essentially the outer swampland of the grand estate that belonged to girls like Sonia Parker.

There she was. She saw Carly, all of a sudden, slinking by on the other side of the hallway like a frightened rodent, attempting to pass undetected. But that was not possible in the heightened awareness that buzzed through the hallways in the electric half hour before first period. Just as Carly attempted to pass unnoticed, one of the popular girls who was standing in a circle near the far wall turned to talk to another girl and bashed Carly with her oversized shoulder bag. Everyone in the circle laughed.

"Oops. Sorry. Didn't see you there," the girl with the shoulder bag said.

It was one of those things the popular kids did on the pretense of innocence, just to amuse their friends. Danielle had always found it disgusting. And yet, suddenly she saw the humor in it. She put her fingers to her lips and tried not to laugh too. Then she shook herself. What was happening to her?

A commotion caught her attention. She turned to see Bethany Myers, the most supremely popular girl in school, looking frantically into her purse and her pockets. She held up her wrist. "Oh no! I've lost my charm!"

Danielle blinked. Was Bethany talking about the charm that she had found in a puddle on her way to school? What were the chances? But she did walk the same route as Bethany—which had long been a source of anxiety. Perhaps it was the very same.

As she watched Bethany searching her things, something very odd happened. Two football players standing nearby began to imitate Bethany with mock histrionics. They flapped their hands in a caricature imitation of her. "Oh me, oh my! I've lost my charm!"

The other kids exploded into laughter and began flapping their hands and talking in fake girlie talk too.

Bethany turned scarlet.

It made no sense. On any normal day, everyone treated Bethany like she walked on water. But today, the girl quickly scuttled off in the same manner as Carly, adhering to the wall of lockers and fleeing like a second-class citizen. What was going on?

In the next moment, Lorelai Bishop, another girl who was a 10 on the Whimden High popularity Richter scale, looped her arm through Danielle's. "Oh my God," she said. "Can you believe Bethany, that sniveling little twerp?"

Evidently it was a rhetorical question. Lorelai pulled her along in the direction of the coffee kiosk. "I'm just dying to tell you about the party on Saturday night. I can't believe you couldn't make it. Everyone was asking about you."

Danielle smiled. "Shut up! Really?"

Had those words just come out of her mouth? Had she just told one of the most popular and dangerous girls at Whimden High to shut up? Her mind reeled.

"Seriously, girlfriend. No party is complete without you."

A boy in a wrinkled T-shirt stepped up to the coffee counter to get a napkin from the dispenser and brushed past Danielle. She was so captivated by this new world order that she barely noticed. But Lorelai did.

"Hey, twit!" she shouted at the boy, giving him a shove so that he nearly fell. "How about respecting Danielle's personal space?"

The boy's face turned ashen and for a moment Danielle wondered if he was going to cry. He had that look about him. She didn't recognize him, but he seemed like the kind of guy she would befriend under normal circumstances. It occurred to her that she might actually be experiencing a psychotic episode of some kind.

"Sorry," he said in the weak tone of the miserable and the tormented. "Won't happen again."

"It had better not," Lorelai said. Then she turned back to Danielle. "Hey, I've got to get to class. I'll see you at lunch, hon!"

Hon? This was an alternate reality, certainly. Gone was her sense of foreboding. Even if this was some kind of bizarre dream, she was going to enjoy it while it lasted.

Her first class of the day was a test of her theory that she had awakened a new person, with actual friends in high places and a social standing she had never dreamed could be hers. She walked in expecting to sit in the last row, as usual, but that row was filled with zitty boys, girls who couldn't afford the latest fashions, and Carly. There were no empty seats. The only spot available was smack in the middle of the classroom. Dead center. The spot reserved for the most popular kid, whomever it may be in that particular class.

She looked around expecting to see scowls, but instead everyone was smiling bashfully at her as if she might be a queen. Everyone except for those in the back row, who were in fact scowling. Carly was in that mix. She and Carly were evidently not friends in the new world order.

"Glad you could join us, Danielle," Mr. Folsom said. In the old days with her prior status, this would have caused waves of snickering, but not today. Not this Danielle. For her there was a respectful silence.

It only lasted a moment until Folsom decided she was the perfect candidate to use as an example. This was the very reason few people were ever late to his class.

"I know everyone loves civics quizzes," he was saying. "Ms. Portola. Since you've captured my attention this morning, let's start with you in our pop quiz." A smirk fluttered across his lips, and she could see that her standing with Folsom too had changed. She was a good student. Just the type he liked. But not now. Not today. Today he had her pegged as one of the in-crowd girls who could not be bothered to open a textbook.

"Ms. Portola," he continued. "I hope you're alert this morning. Can you tell us which branch of government has the power to make laws?"

There was a slight gasp amongst those around her. Evidently they believed she had been set up for failure. But it was child's play.

"That would be the legislative branch," she said. If he thought he was going to catch her off guard, he was going to be disappointed. Danielle loved civics.

A general sigh of relief was emitted by the class.

"Fine, fine. Alright let's see how you do with one more. Which branch is the U.S. military commander in chief?"

Again, she was stunned at the simplicity of the question. Folsom seemed certain Danielle was going to give some air headed answer, and she almost hated to disappoint him. But this wasn't her day to play dumb. "The executive branch. Of course."

Folsom's eyes fluttered. He pursed his lips and took a few paces across the floor. Clearly, as one of the popular girls she was expected to be out socializing in the evenings, not doing homework and actually learning things. She was not following the protocol.

"Very impressive, Ms. Portola," Folsom said. And though he had a smile on his face like someone who is genuinely pleased, the bead of sweat at his temple suggested otherwise. "Since you're doing so well, let's see if you can do three for three."

She nodded. She felt all eyes on her. Under normal circumstances, she would be withering beneath those watchful eyes, but instead she sensed her classmates were on her side.

"So. For the third pop quiz question today, which branch of the U.S. government can review laws for their constitutionality?"

She shook her head, wishing for a question that was actually difficult. Perhaps thinking this meant she could not come up with the answer, her classmates inhaled and held their collective breath. Mr. Folsom stared at her, as if willing her to fail, a grin growing wider and wider on his face.

"That is, of course, the judicial branch."

The grin left Folsom's face. "Quite right."

"Wow!" the girl next to her said. And a guy she had always admired from afar uttered, "Good job, Danielle! Man, who knew?"

She wanted to revel in the praise, but that spidey sense she'd felt earlier that something was off was rearing its ugly head again. If she accepted hollow victories, wasn't she doing a disservice to herself? The chaos of emotions she felt clouded her ability to sort this out, but she vowed to think more about it later. For now, she smiled meekly at those around her, both charmed and disturbed that they were so surprised about her knowledge.

"Babe," a boy's voice said as she left class. "I've been looking for you everywhere."

"Oh?"

She flushed as it registered that the voice came from Kevin Sodermeier, and he was talking to her. Kevin was an absolute dream. She had admired him from afar for two years, since Freshman year. He and Bethany were dating. Everyone knew that. Was he actually her boyfriend in this alternate reality?

He swung her around and then pressed her against a locker and gave her a deep kiss, tongue and all. She accepted this – it was part of the deal, right? – but at the same time she felt a little repulsed.

"Wow," she said, pushing him away to a safe distance. "Let me catch my breath."

"That's not what you said on Saturday night."

Oh God. She hadn't, had she? No, she couldn't have! But wait. She would know. She was sure of it. And that absolutely had not happened. Not even in this bizarre dream, or whatever it was. She felt the heat in her cheeks.

"Relax," he said. "I know you're not ready. But you will be. Soon." He leaned in to kiss her on the neck. Then he nibbled on her ear.

She felt hot. Confused. Unsure whether or not she liked this. His hand slipped around her waist and down, and then he squeezed her rear, pulling her pelvis toward his. She couldn't breathe.

"Kevin," she said, pushing him back. "My gosh. We're going to get detention for PDA, don't you think? We'd better..."

"Who cares? I just want everyone to know you're mine." He leaned in again. "And you're going to be mine... all the way. Girls like you don't put it off forever, you know. We just need to find the right time and place."

She tried to smile.

Just then Carly walked by on the other side of the hall. She stared at the floor as she walked, clearly afraid of being caught watching them making out.

"Carly!" Danielle called. "I'll walk with you to class."

Carly looked at her, mortified. Kevin gave one more squeeze of her butt and let her go.

"Listen, Carly. What's going on around here? It's like someone has cast a spell on this place."

"I really don't know what you're talking about," Carly said. She wouldn't make eye contact.

Danielle thought about Bethany – who had always been so popular – being taunted for losing her charm earlier that day.

That had been the first sign that things were off. "I mean, did you see what happened to Bethany this morning?"

"Yeah," Carly said. "I did. And it was terrible. Bethany's my friend, okay? I don't get why everyone picks on her. Why can't you and your mean friends just leave her alone? You're such horrible people." With that, she stomped off down a corridor.

Danielle was losing her mind. That was the only sensible explanation at this point. She and Carly weren't friends anymore. Bethany wasn't popular. And Carly was defending her. Meanwhile, she was evidently palsy-walsies with Lorelai Bishop, Kevin was her boyfriend, and everyone expected her to be an airhead. This, she thought – all of this – is what gave her the feeling that jungle drums were booming a distant, rhythmic threat. And it wasn't going to end well.

She dreaded strolling into the cafeteria at lunch, but there Lorelai was to loop an arm in hers again and steer her toward the popular girls' table. All the girls were there. Sonia Parker, Lorelai, and another girl named Patrice Watkins whom everyone expected to be crowned as prom queen in the spring. She was very pretty. If you cared for the Barbie princess look, that is. And she had a Ken doll boyfriend to match. Danielle had always wondered what life would be like if she had been graced with splendid good looks at birth.

And then she found out. Because in this new world order, whatever beauty she came by naturally had given her the rights to the popular girls' table, and a lot of envious looks from the people at tables nearby.

Patrice leaned across the table and touched her hand. "I love how you did your hair today, Danielle! But you always look so amazing."

She rolled her eyes and shrugged with a meek smile. What were you supposed to do? She tried to remember how she had seen Bethany behave before they traded places. Bethany had composure. She was not only beautiful to look at, but she always seemed poised, like someone who had actually been to a professional charm school.

"Listen, girls," Lorelai said. "I've got something top secret to tell you. And it concerns you, Danielle." She looked around at each of them with the wide eyes of someone who is nearly bursting with the most precious secret.

"Tell, tell," Sonia said. "Does it have to do with that hunk boyfriend of hers?"

"It does," Lorelai said, drawing out the words, the way a talking snake might.

"The anticipation is literally killing me," Patrice said.

Danielle wanted to educate her on the meaning of the word "literal," but thought better of it.

"So," Lorelai said. "Friday night is the big game, right? And of course we're going to have our usual tailgate party with Eddy and his boys."

Danielle wracked her brain, and then remembered that Eddy was the captain of the varsity soccer team, and a good friend of Kevin's. It made sense that they all tailgated with the girls at the football games. She began to dread what was coming next.

"And it's going to be the absolute perfect opportunity for you..." Lorelai drawled, pointing at Danielle, "to have some intimate time with Kevin."

When Danielle started to speak, Lorelai raised her hand. "Don't thank me, honey. I totally owe you a favor since you helped me to hook up with Eddy. It's all arranged. Once the festivities are underway, you and Kevin will slip off to Eddy's camper van, which he is going to borrow from his parents for the evening on the pretense of using it for the tailgate party. Capeesh?"

Danielle thought she might pass out. She fanned her face with her hand.

"Oh my God, she's so cute," Sonia said to the other girls. Then she turned to Danielle. "Sweetie, everyone's nervous their first time. Don't you worry. Kevin will treat you right."

"Plus," Patrice said, "you really need to join our little club. You've waited long enough."

Danielle got up. She needed air. She was starting to feel like Dorothy in the Wizard of Oz. She wished for magic words, like "There's no place like home."

All the girls got up at the same time. "Good idea," Lorelai said. "Let's all take a walk."

"I know where we should go," Patrice said in a sing-song voice. And she steered the group of girls down the hallway toward the library.

"What do you have in mind?" Sonia asked. "Have you taken a sudden interest in books?"

Patrice laughed. "Don't be ridiculous. This is so much better. I just happen to know the study habits of two very annoying book worms. And they should be leaving the library right about..."

Just then the door to the library swung open and Carly and Bethany emerged.

"...now."

Danielle winced. These two people – her former best friend, and the girl whose place in the school social hierarchy she had usurped – were the last ones she would like to interact with right now. They were in the middle of some hushed political discussion and seemed to be debating the pros and cons of the filibuster system. But they stopped cold when they saw Sonia, Patrice, Lorelai and Danielle, who quickly encircled them.

With a swift motion of her arm, Patrice knocked Carly's armload of books to the ground. "Oops," she said, putting her fingers to her lips in the manner of a stage actor.

Danielle sucked in her breath. She blanched at the idea that she had found it funny when another girl slammed Carly with her backpack that morning. Only a creep and a coward would find that humorous. She wanted to kneel down and help to pick up the books, but she could not. Even now, she was carried along by the crowd mentality of the popular girls, who were walking in a slow, menacing circle around Carly and Bethany. She was one of them. A vulture, feasting on the damaged egos of others.

"We can let you go in peace, of course," Lorelai said. "We only command a small price. It's not much."

Danielle looked around. Were there no hall monitors? Not a teacher or a librarian? Was absolutely everyone in the school in the cafeteria? She looked up at the corners of the hallway and to her relief saw security cameras. But her relief was short-lived because she saw Patrice glance up at them too, and she realized these girls were well aware they were being watched. It was all a game of posturing and intimidation. A game to see what they could make their victims do.

Lorelai looked around at her friends. "What shall it be, ladies?"

"Oh I have the perfect thing," Sonia said. "As soon as one of the fine lads attending this institution comes down this hall, you will both lift up your blouses and show your breasts. And I do mean show them. You're going to have to take at least one of those precious melons out of the holster and show it off."

"Perfect," Patrice said. "Then we won't have to hold you down and take your shirts off for you. And you won't be forced to run home half naked. Win win!"

The look on Carly's and Bethany's faces was heart wrenching. Both of them looked pale in the weird light of the fluorescent hallway bulbs. The lighting near the library had always been dim, and the windows inside were high and small, perhaps by design to protect the books from damaging light and heat.

Lorelai gently pushed Danielle toward the two girls in the middle of the circle. "Now, Danielle, here is what we like to call our 'enforcer.' You may not know this, but the girl has a mean streak a mile deep. And she is prepared to do whatever it takes to help you two comply. I certainly hope she doesn't have to use the knife she keeps hidden in her waistband!"

Lorelai winked at Danielle. It was sick. It was wrong. Just terribly terribly wrong. She wanted to cry.

And then it happened. Two guys came walking down the hallway, tossing a basketball back and forth. They hadn't noticed the girls, though as soon as they did, Danielle knew what was going to happen. Sonia, Patrice, and Lorelai were going to step away from Carly and Bethany, and Danielle would need to give

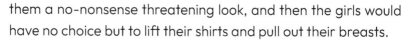

them a no-nonsense threatening look, and then the girls would have no choice but to lift their shirts and pull out their breasts.

Think. Think. She could call for help. Or yell at the boys to look the other way. No, she'd be pegged as a traitor. What was the punishment for that? But she thought of the tailgate party on Friday night, and what awaited her then. Perhaps sacrificing herself now was a better deal.

Then she thought of the charm—the tiny, seemingly innocent trinket in her pocket that had launched this bizarre chain of events. She reached into her pocket and found it there. It felt cool in her hand, yet it warmed instantly to her touch as if it had some knowledge of the weird magic it possessed.

Just as the boys came near enough that they stopped tossing the ball to step around the girls, she leaned over and placed it in Bethany's hand, closing her fingers around it.

"I think you lost this," she said, looking into Bethany's eyes where she saw an intricately entwined combination of fear and brave composure.

Suddenly Bethany stood up straight, as if infused with strength and personal conviction. "Back off, okay?" she said. "You're sort of in my personal space."

She was back. The switch was complete.

Danielle smiled. There was no bite to what Bethany said. She was just playing the required role of a popular girl hanging out with these fashionable hooligans. And for the first time, Danielle saw how different from them Bethany was. She had fallen in with these girls, but she was not truly one of them. Perhaps she even felt trapped in her little clique.

"Hey," Lorelai said, glowering now at Carly and Danielle. "We had an agreement, I believe." She held a hand up to hold the boys at bay, and they had stopped walking obediently. No one defied Lorelai.

"I don't think so," Danielle said. "You had a sick and twisted demand, but that doesn't mean we agreed to it."

Lorelai stepped toward her. "Excuse me?"

Danielle had never felt so brave. "It's not happening. And guess what, brainiac. You can't actually hurt us because we're all on school security cams right now. Nice try. But we're not your bitches."

She looped her arm through Carly's. Carly was warm and familiar by her side, and Danielle could smell the flower aroma that always seemed to accompany her, as if she just stepped out of a field of lavender.

She began to lead Carly away, but then she stopped and leaned toward Bethany whispering, "You don't have to do anything you don't really want to do. Not ever."

Then she said to the boys, "You guys heading this way? Great. So are we." Now she and Carly began walking in step with the boys as they moved away toward the school's corridors and classrooms, as if there was always a place to go and a way to find something better in the old House of Horrors that was Whimden High.

Johnny Matherne

Draguignan - France

I am graduate student (English/Creative Writing track) at the University of Louisiana, Monroe.

2. Holy Thursday

I remember later thinking that perhaps I'd bitten off a little more than I could chew. Two of my classmates had been leaving class early for a couple of weeks and I wondered why only they should be so lucky. I had no particular affinity for class or our teacher, so I asked. When told me they were learning to be altar boys, I immediately wanted to be an altar boy myself, not quite yet understanding that I'd have to be in the front of the church, with the priest, performing, so to speak, for all to see. I just drew great satisfaction in thinking that I could get out of class an hour early.

"Tommy, an altar boy must be ready to serve God and Jesus at all times. Are you sure?" asked Sister Mary Rosalyn. I put on my best sincere face, head tilted down a little, eyes looking up, and replied, "Yes, Sister." An off she went, straight out of the classroom to Father Folse's office, informing him of the good news.

I cannot remember the month, but it must have been April, or close to it, because I received my assignment, and it was to be Holy Thursday. Not a 6:30 am weekday mass, which would have been a good way to ease into holy servitude—those only ran 30 minutes—or even a Saturday evening mass where the few members of the flock in attendance would have their keys in hand, jingling in anticipation for the end of the gospel, ready to hustle out the door after communion, not giving any real attention to what was going on in front of the church. No, there would be no warm-up or practice game. My debut would be during one of the biggest events on the liturgical calendar.

Center stage was not for me. For one of my birthday parties—I think my fifth—my mom hired a clown. The clown did the required balloon animals and then called me up in front of everyone. He got down on one knee, looked deep into my eyes, and started to sing a slow, birthday-themed song. Everyone fell silent as this character serenaded me. My grandmothers clutched their chests and whispered how sweet they thought all of this to be. I didn't know where to look—I certainly didn't want to look into his eyes or watch his mouth, with all that white makeup outlined in black moving and stretching every which way while he sang. I didn't know where to put my hands or if everyone could see how hot my face had become. I also wondered, for some reason, what my dad thought of this scene. And I wanted to run.

I'd had a similar spotlight experience the year prior to my fourth-grade year. Sister Mary Jude, my third-grade teacher, lived off of Biblical verses and fed on the souls of children, souls that she extracted with a wooden ruler or a stick or her hands. She once recounted a biblical tale involving a character I can't remember, but his only aspiration in life, it seemed, was to sing songs of praise to the Lord. She made sure that we knew that this character didn't sing rock 'n roll, and he didn't write love songs to women, but only songs to God offered up in piety. We too should aspire, she reminded us, to serve God, and no matter what we grew up to be, we should find a way to intertwine profession and faith. And so she surveyed the class.

"Michelle, what do you want to be when you grow up?" she asked.

"I want to be a nurse," she replied.

"Why?"

"So I can help people," she said, clearly on board with the program.

"Very good," said Sister Mary Jude. "Steven, what do you want to be when you grow up?"

"I want to be a firefighter, because they help people, too."

"Very good," she said, pleased with another wholesome response.

As luck would have it, I had spent the weekend prior at my Uncle Billy and Aunt Susie's house. My five cousins and I were talking about what we wanted to be when we grew up, and I said that I didn't know. We had just finished watching *Trapper John, M.D.*, and my oldest cousin, Janie, suggested that maybe I could be a doctor because they make a lot of money. So when it was my turn:

"I want to be a doctor because they make a lot of money."

There were seconds of silence that felt like minutes, and the look on Sister Mary Jude's face would have made you think that the air was filled not with silence but sulfur.

"You see, class," she finally started, after breathing again, "Tommy Bourgeois worships false idols. He worships money instead of God, much like Moses' brother, Aaron, who worshiped a golden calf. And we all know how that turned out. Tommy, before lunch, you need to say an extra decade of the rosary as penance."

My classmates, company men and women, one and all, let out an "Ooooooooohhhhh!", some pointing at me and some holding their hands over their mouths while giggling.

Sister Mary Jude had once even told me that every time I was mischievous, perhaps Jesus would be receiving another lashing with a whip. For a child who had all the behavioral characteristics of most other children of the same age, this was all a bit much. My shoulders surely were too narrow to bear the responsibility of the further suffering of the Lord's only Son! Wasn't He supposed to now be in Paradise anyway?

And after all of this, I had somehow managed to voluntarily put myself in a position where, on Holy Thursday, people would do what I hated most—look at me.

Sister Mary Rosalyn had told me to report to the church the Wednesday before so that I could meet with Father Gregoire and go over the particulars of Holy Thursday mass. Holy Thursday mass lasted longer than any regular service and had many moving parts. It required four altar boys instead of three—we had to get it ironed out, nice and smooth, before the big show.

My dad got me to the church early on that cloudy Wednesday evening. Father Gregoire must have heard the heavy black double doors slam shut behind us because he waddled out of the rectory seconds after we came in. I tried not to look at him as he walked towards us, his mouth breathing growing louder as he got closer. He was younger and rounder than the other priests, with his hair permed in tight curls on top of his head. The top two buttons of his black shirt were open, and his white collar was not around his neck but stuck into his shirt pocket, looking much like the popsicle stick the doctor used to hold down your tongue while looking in your throat.

Father Gregoire put his hands on his knees and got his face close to mine, asking, "And how are we today, young man?" He was close enough that I could start to count the whiskers above his lip—I could almost see the coffee and cigarettes through the big gap between his two front teeth. "Good," I said, trying not to make it too obvious that I was backing away. He shook hands with my dad, and I did not pay attention as they talked, as Father Gregoire made me uncomfortable. I ran my fingertips over one of the jagged, rugged crosses carved on the outside of all the pews, and studied the tall, imposing stained glass windows. All of the colorful images in the windows depicted something from the Bible and were framed in small white circles. The hues, however, were dark, and even in the daytime, the interior of the church had a feeling of the evening. The section of wall between each window held up elaborate sculptures of the Stations of the Cross. I tried to lose myself in the colors and the intricate designs and tried to read the inscriptions on the sculptures, written in the language of my grandparents:

Jésus est condamné.

Jésus est chargé de la croix.

Father Gregoire started his instruction once the rest of the team had arrived. Our duties on the altar seemed to be the same altar administrata as any other service—ring the bells, pour the water, pour the wine, and the like. It was the meandering up and down the aisles that would be different. The oldest boy, an eighth-grader named Jean, was a Holy Thursday veteran. He had it easy. His duties mostly required him to remain in place at the altar. The Trosclair twins and I had to accompany the priest as he splashed the congregation with holy water. Tim's responsibility would be to hold the bucket of water and Terry would lead the way with the big crucifix. As for me, I had to rattle the little gold smoking ball, I guess to make sure everyone could smell the incense burning inside it. All in all, it didn't sound like a difficult task. Even better, we learned that Father Frye would conduct the mass. Father Frye, a schoolyard favorite, always spoke to me about baseball and often led students in cheers in an effort to foment school spirit. His fiery sermons went unmatched—even the televangelists paled in comparison. Perhaps he'd draw enough attention to himself that no one would notice me.

My aunts and my grandmothers took nearly no interest in any of my extracurricular activities. Once, I'd asked my Aunt Theresa if she'd like to come to one of my baseball games, as I was finding my stride as a second baseman. She joked that she'd rather watch the grass grow. But once the word got out that I'd be involved in some sort of official Catholic act, the aunts and the grandmothers appeared en masse with Sunday best dresses and rosaries in hand. They all came to our house hours before the service would start. My mom arranged a bunch of chairs in the living room in a semi-circle so they could all sit and cluck about how proud they were of me as they drank coffee and snacked on cake and divinity fudge. My mom ushered me towards the semi-circle so each one could comment on my outfit and ask me questions about what being an altar boy meant to me. My Aunt Debra and my Aunt Del even suggested that this might have been the beginning of my path to the priesthood, and oh how both of my grandmothers delighted in that prospect! I became more and more focused on the fact that more and more faces would be focused on me before long, far more than those in my living room. My guts started to bubble and I ran to the bathroom. I didn't want to leave, and my dad eventually had to pull me out.

We climbed into my dad's little yellow Ford Courier, backed out of the driveway, and headed for the church. I mixed the dried dirt on the floor with the toes and heels of my brown Earth shoes. I glanced at an empty, crinkled Kool cigarette wrapper that lay next to the stick shift. My dad's truck always reeked of the stale smell of cigarette smoke and dust but that day it went unnoticed.

"Tommy Boy, what are you so scared of?" my dad asked me as we turned the first curve we came to on the River Road, his black hair tousled by the wind.

"I don't know. Everybody's going to see me. Was you nervous when you was an altar boy?"

"I don't quite remember. I guess I probably was a little. I was always with my buddies, though. We had to answer the priest in Latin. Just think if you had to do that. You ain't got it so bad."

"What if I mess up?" I asked.

"Well, so what? Just keep goin'. Ain't nobody gonna notice anyway, I bet."

I took in his words while watching the levee and the trees behind it go by. I let a few minutes pass and then, aside from this fear of being watched and judged by the masses, I told my Dad of something else that had been on my mind.

"What if I get in trouble?" I asked.

"In trouble? With who?"

"With Sister Mary Jude or Sister Mary Rosalyn, or with you, or Momma, or the priest."

It did not take us long to get to the church. We pulled into the church parking lot and parked. My dad put the truck in neutral and pulled the parking brake with a powerful yank of his once-a-quarterback arm like he always did. I wondered when the day would come that he'd pull it straight out of its housing. He then propped his left elbow on top of the steering wheel, squared his square shoulders to me, and looked at me with a smile.

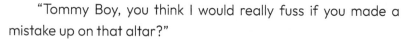
"Tommy Boy, you think I would really fuss if you made a mistake up on that altar?"

"I don't know," I replied. "Shit, boy, I don't even go to church," he said. "I'm just going today. And I promise, your Mom wouldn't fuss you just for a mistake, you know? If you were cutting up, or drinking wine in the rectory, that's one thing, but just a mistake? That ain't no big deal."

I started to smile a little as I rubbed my hands up and down on my thighs a couple of times. Sometimes the old man's blue eyes could be cold and pierce you, but sometimes you'd look at them and they would be just what you needed. My old man was tough, but sometimes, well, he wasn't. "What about Sister Mary Jude?" I asked. "I feel like I'm always in trouble with her without even trying, and she's not even my teacher anymore."

"Don't worry about her too much. Like you said, she's not even your teacher anymore. Besides, them nuns go without, that's her problem."

"They go without what?" I asked.

"They just do, don't worry about it," he said, cracking a smile. "Just do your best."

And so it was. I agreed to do my best and try not to be so nervous.

We entered the big white church. The church had been built over 100 years ago and for so long I'd heard so many people comment on its beauty. Many years later, as an adult, I would agree that it was impressive, but as a child, it was just big and old. It smelled like the books in our old school library, and it had other old building smells that I recognized but couldn't identify. The cedar pews didn't smell of cedar anymore, and the years of repeated finishing had rendered them black. I even knew of their bitter taste, because once, while kneeling, I had placed my mouth on the pew in front of me, and our principal, Sister Mary André, slapped me on the back of the head, giving me a taste of over 100 years of varnish.

Red carpet ran down the wide middle aisle (*Look, they rolled it out for us again!* My grandpa would joke every Sunday) and there were long pews to the left and the right. At the end of the long pews, on each side, ran another aisle, and then shorter pews, and those bumped up against the walls. We found Father Frye standing in the smaller aisle to the right, near the front, talking with Jean.

"Hi, John, how are you?" he asked my Dad as they shook hands.

"I'm doing well, Father. I think we got the boy here all ready to go."

"There's our second-bagger. How are you doing, Tommy?" Father Frye asked me, remembering that I played second base.

"I'm ok, I guess."

"Just ok? Gonna be a piece of cake, alright?"

I stuck a finger through one of my belt loops and gave him a little nod, and he gave me a thumbs up.

My Dad put his hand on the top of my head. "I'm gonna go get your Mom and your grandmothers," he said.

"Ok," I replied.

Father Frye told Jean and me to get ready, so I followed Jean into the rectory to put on my red altar boy gown with the white thing that went on top. The rectory had a smell just like the rest of the church, maybe even stronger, with many old books with yellowed pages on the shelves. The room was square and it always struck me as odd, because the exterior of the church where the rectory stood was rounded. There was on the far wall a square picture of the Virgin holding the baby Christ, set in a round frame but a bit off-center. Jean, having dressed quicker than me, started to prepare the wine and the hosts, and decided to take a little sip for himself.

"Hey, you. Want some of this, you?" he asked. Jean had heavy eyelids that almost covered half of his brown eyes and curly hair that brushed his eyelashes. At school, he made me uncomfortable—a different way than Father Gregoire—but still uncomfortable, and he could be seen almost regularly sitting in a chair outside Sister Mary Andre's office.

"Nah . . . no . . . I don't think so," I said. My father's recent list of transgressions was only minutes old in my mind, and I thought it best to be mindful.

"Well, nobody better find out, you hear?"

"Ok," I said as he took another sip.

The Trosclair twins arrived. They didn't say hi to Jean. I couldn't be sure, but maybe the two sixth graders had had a run-in with him in the schoolyard, as they kept their distance. They didn't say hi to me either and just started to get dressed.

When it was time to start, we exited the rectory and walked around the exterior of the church to the front entrance. Father Frye waited with the two readers and the deacon. He put us in a tight formation like fighter jets headed for a mission. Terry was out front with the crucifix, followed by Tim and Jean, side by side, and then me. The two readers and the deacon were last, and Father Frye then put himself at the front of the procession. The notes of the big pipe organ started to blare only seconds after we were set, and our procession started off down the center aisle. Father Frye held the gospel high, and we walked with our religious garb brushing the floor, our shoes barely peeking out from under them. No turning back now.

My dad had once told me how nervous he could get before a football game, but after the first play, the nerves were gone. I felt the same way once the service began. I focused not on the congregation but more on making sure that I didn't trip over myself, and once at the altar, we all took our positions with no distress.

The service progressed with this holy word and that one, and a prayer to whomever until it was time to walk among the congregation, blessing and cleansing with holy water and releasing the rich smell of smokey incense in order to do whatever it was that it did. I lit the incense inside the little gold ball on a chain at the altar (*It is called a censer*, as Father Gregoire had once corrected me), and we took up our positions again. This time, Terry was at the front with the crucifix, followed by me and my increasingly hot censer, then Father Frye and Tim with the water. We started down the aisle toward the main entrance.

At practice, Father Gregoire had shown me how to swing the censer. He held the end of the chain with his left hand towards the floor and ran his right hand up the chain a little past halfway. He pushed with his right hand just enough to get the censer swinging forward and backward, and each time it would swing back, it would clank against the chain. It looked much like the way someone would configure a yo-yo for a trick. And so on that day, I did the same. Before long, my censer moved back and forth with a distinctive rhythm, and Father Frye splashed the holy water left and right with a rhythm of his own, all while

we walked in formation with military precision down the center aisle.

We arrived at the last pew and went around to the aisle on the left. We moved back toward the altar and about halfway there, I decided that I needed to reposition my hands. I repositioned my right hand, however, a little too close to the censer.

"Ah ya yie!" I shouted as I let go of the hot chain, letting the burning censer bounce off of the red carpet.

The pain in my fingers was sharp, but I could not leave the burning ball on the floor, so I picked the chain up, careful not to grab so close this time. I stood up. The procession had stopped. Father Frye's splashing had stopped. And everyone in the church faced my direction. I did not know what to do, so I straightened up, pursed my lips, and started to swing my censer again.

"Is everything ok?" Father Frye whispered, but I just kept swinging, so he got the procession moving again.

I wish I could say that the rest of the service went on without issue, but I missed my bell-ringing cues later on. I also tripped once, and by the time the service was over, I just wanted to get out of the church, abandoning all worries that I'd get in trouble for a poor performance.

After the mass, I found my family waiting outside for me. My Granny Bourgeois, determined to keep my spirits up, reminded me that it was my first time, and told me that she didn't think I'd made mistakes on purpose. Just as I started to feel as if I'd come to grips with my errors, Sister Mary Jude walked up to us with her missal in one hand and her rosary in the other.

"Why hello, Philomena, I was just telling Tommy Boy how well we thought he did today," my Granny Bourgeois said. My Granny Boo always wore a smile and did not like confrontation. She never spoke ill of anyone. Today, her face was stern and void of that smile. I also, in my mind, tried to process her calling the nun "Philomena". I'd always thought her name was just Mary Jude.

"Well, a little more concentration and he wouldn't have made mistakes," the nun said.

"It was his first time in front of all those people. Wouldn't you say he still did well?" asked my Granny Boo.

"But when in the service of the Lord, one should . . ."

"Wouldn't you say he still did well . . . Philomena?" asked my other grandmother, interrupting at a higher octave than everyone else. In stark contrast to my Granny Boo, Grandmother Zeringue never wore a smile, could be quite critical of others, and insisted that we address her as strictly "Grandmother", as she deemed other such nicknames for elders to be childish and inappropriate.

Sister Mary Jude lifted her head slightly, looked at my Granny Boo, and then only glanced at my Grandmother Zeringue. I looked behind me where my father stood, hands on hips, his feet spread slightly wider than shoulder length. The frigidity of his blue eyes had returned, though they were not trained on me. My mother had one hand inside the bend of his arm while holding her purse with the other, her expression matching my father's. Sister Mary Jude looked at them as well. And then she had no further platitudes to offer.

Sister Mary Rosalyn approached, her long white habit barely touching the ground, and I'm sure she must have at least seen, and maybe heard, this brief exchange from a distance. She wanted no part of it, as she gently took Sister Mary Jude by the arm and said, "Come, Sister." And they walked away, through the rectangular parking lot and into the convent.

Dalton Mire

Bradenton, Florida - United States

He has published several short stories and two novels

3. Another Jungle Bungle

Thucketa, thucketa, thucketa . . . Dex kicked me, "Mick, we're here." Snapped awake, I peeked over the edge of the whirlybird door with my gloved hand on a line that seemed much too thin to hold my two-hundred-and-ten-pound camo-covered carcass. This flying elevator was about to drop me on the ground floor of the jungle below. Stepping into nothingness with a sinking feeling in my gut, the cable jerked tight, and the winch whined from my weight. Thundering blades hit me with a downdraft, and my world spun. My buddy grabbed the cable to save me from a dizzying descent.

How many times have I done this? Too many to count. *Hopefully, there won't be anyone shooting at me this time.* Flying bullets added excitement to dull drops in Columbia. My old fatigues do not meet military standards but were the only things that were clean. My mismatched outfit combines a top of leafy green and brown forest camo and a bottom of desert sand trousers. *I look like a tree.* With a knapsack on my back, another on my chest, and a duffle bag attached to my black-booted foot, the ominous wilderness waited below. *Well, at least, whatever was down there.*

A big round hole in the canopy opened off to my right, but unfortunately, a gust of wind blew me away from an easy landing. After smashing through the leaves and limbs covering this sauna, the hot, humid jungle air blasted my body like the devil's own breath. The bag hanging from my foot got caught on a branch and forced me to shout "Stop" into my tactical headset to keep me from flipping upside down.

Dangling in a treetop, struggling with this stupid duffle challenged my upbringing—Mama taught me not to cuss. With her scowling image hovering over my shoulder, I prayed for help from any god who happened to be listening. After great exhortations and help from above, the demon sack surrendered.

Free at last, free at last, Dex slowed my descent and prevented me from crashing into Mother Earth. With legs bent when boots slammed into the jungle floor, my butt did not hit the ground. *Hey, I am a professional.* The overwhelming stink of rotting vegetation assaulted my nose as I unhooked the line and watched it zip through the canopy. On the way, it disturbed several bright red and green parrots who squawked to remind me I was alone in a creature-infested jungle.

✳✳✳

Dexter Perkins organized this safari. He is big and Black and once played linebacker for the Edmonton Elks. He called me early one morning and disturbed my hangover, "Ken Burwell wants to know if a precocious boy has discovered a lost city in the Yucatan jungle."

"And why do I care?"

"Burwell's the richest man in Canada."

I rubbed my swollen eyes and said, "Oh, that Burwell. Can't make it. I'm coaching youth league hockey. Got a game."

"Mick, I need you. Remember, I saved your life in the jungle. No bullets this time, just plenty of cash."

My father cautioned me never to volunteer, but something has always made me weigh profit against danger. My survival has depended on a wink and a prayer, yet Dex's sentiment evoked dark memories. I owed him. Besides, an adventure would rescue me from the boredom of surfing the Internet and might fill my pathetically thin wallet with loonies. Helping a kid find his dream was right up my alley.

On the tarmac in Mexico City, our jungle bird turned out to be a C-47 Chinook that had seen better days. Dex and I loaded the gear and welcomed the two archaeologists who formed the rest of the "Burwell Expedition." These grave robbers, true to their profession, were dressed in the required khaki shirts, shorts, and loose jackets with big pockets. And, of course, cameras dangled from their necks. Doctor Ulla Anderson turned out to be a tall blond who immediately looked down on me. She had to be at least 6' 2," and on a good day, I am a short 5' 11. *She'd better duck when she exits this flying fan in the jungle.*

A red felt cowgirl hat was precariously perched on top of her head and ponytail at a jaunty angle. This flimsy chapeau had "Calgary Stampede" embroidered across the front in a chain of white cursive letters, and she used the white chin cord to hold up the brim on each side. Doc Anderson introduced herself, "I'm a professor at McGill University."

The college set has always left me feeling like a mushroom in manure. Especially when she shook my hand and asked, "Where did you go to school?"

My retort, "My classroom was a fireplace in a small log cabin three miles below the Arctic Circle. The Holy Bible was my only textbook, and my majors were dog sleds and caribou."

She acknowledged my impudence with a slight sneer and introduced me to the next khaki-clad explorer, "This is Doctor Stanley Livingstone. We are colleagues in the same department."

I, of course, greeted him with, "Dr. Livingstone, I presume."

He shook his head in disbelief and told me, "Unfortunately, you're not the first to honor me with that trite welcome. My parents loved African explorers. My first name comes from Henry Stanley, who searched that continent to find Doctor David Livingstone. And, as you obviously know, their meeting coined that historic phrase."

This Livingstone was a short, thin man with a well-trimmed white beard and a tanned bald head. He was one of those guys who looked better without hair. At least he does not have to worry about being scalped by swirling blades when he ran fromed a copter. My only hope was that he brought along a pith helmet to protect his exposed brain from the tropical sun.

Dr. Anderson settled inside on a wooden bench and told me in an excited squeal, "Call me Ulla. This is my first time on a heliocopter."

I grinned, "Just hope it's not your last. Helios are dangerous birds."

Then she asked, "How were you selected for this expedition?"

"The military recruits lonely boys living in the frozen tundra. I jumped at the chance to see the world and get warm. Dex and I served together and make a good team."

Just as the blades started to rotate, Dex nodded to Doc Anderson, "You've got the floor, ma'am."

After a stare that made me sit up straight and pay attention, Ulla rattled through our mission. "In 2016, a 15-year-old, William Gadoury, examined *The Mayan Doomsday Prophecies* and noticed that the location of Mayan cities matched the Mayan star charts, but one city was missing. He theorized that an undiscovered Mayan metropolis existed in the Mexican jungle at that spot. The Canadian Space Agency, NASA, and the Japanese Space Agency used satellites to test this young man's theory. My friend, Armand LaRocque, from the University of New Brunswick studied the imagining results and found a geometric shape at the boy's location that could be a pyramid."

Ulla stopped for a moment to compose herself. Something was wrong. Her face was flushed, and she stuttered, "Mayan . . . Mayan expert, David Stuart, infuriated me when he dismissed this teenager's theory as 'Junk Science.' God, he made me so mad."

She ground her teeth and curled her lip before continuing, "Because of him, other so-called experts in our field have failed to confirm or disprove this boy's discovery. The jealous eunuchs in our profession who hide in the hallowed halls of academia and ignore discoveries made by amateurs really upset me. Our mission is to discover if this young man was right."

Then Dex chimed in, "We will drop in, scout the area for ruins, stay overnight, and get picked up late tomorrow. Easy-peasy, eh? Jungles have creepy-crawly things. Mick and me are the brawn to protect you brains. Mick will drop through the jungle canopy on what might be the top of the pyramid, and we will land in an opening near what could be at the bottom."

***

With my feet firmly planted on the jungle landscape, I looked around and discovered stone blocks under my feet. *I should call up. The team could leave now—the kid was right.*

Standing one level below the top of this man-made mountain, I thought, *might as well be the first of our expedition to scale this stack of stones.* Leaving my packs behind, tangled greenery hindered my progress to the last wall leading to the top. I placed my hand firmly on a tree root to pull myself up, but something was wrong; it moved. I peeked over the top, and a huge snake as thick as my calf stared back. This jungle serpent was brown with yellow streaks running down his sides. He reminded me of a wiener dog with mustard. This impolite bastard stuck his tongue out and thank God, slithered off. I glanced up to thank heaven, *at least he didn't swallow me whole.* I am not scared of much, but snakes are on my shortlist.

A dull bulb flashed in my pedestrian brain, *why not use the steps on my right to climb to the top?* My triumphant ascension was celebrated by waving my fists and arms above my head like "Rocky." Even in the jungle, movies make life more exciting. Leafy branches whacked my face and body as I explored the top and discovered a clearing where the stone blocks were scraped bare. Someone or something had wiped them clean. The steps leading down this side of the pyramid looked brand new. Other feet had been trudging on them. My wide-open orbs searched this steaming green prison for prying eyes as clouds of doom rained down on my soul. *Sorry, it's the movies.* Dramatic recitations have added excitement to my dull world.

After retrieving my gear, each step down the staircase of this steep Turkish bath made every orifice in my body weep. I kept pulling off my blue Toronto Argonauts cap to wipe the sweat from my beaded brow. A small clearing welcomed me at the bottom, and the compass on my wrist made it clear that the rest of the team landed on the other side of the pyramid. After adios-ing the packs, my trusty machete disturbed the jungle countenance as my brawny biceps chopped through the foliage. Exhausted after a few whacks, a game trail saved me. The creatures who created this shortcut forced me to duck-walk down most of the path, but not having to cut through the twisted vines and vegetation silenced my lamentations.

The bright beam in my hand helped me navigate this dark hole, and huge stone blocks led me around the first corner of the pyramid. Intent on saving my eyes from protruding branches, I literally bumped into a jaguar's butt. This Siegfried and Roy-sized cat did not want to rub my leg to get a meal. I was the meal. Eh!

Shocked by my presence in his world, this fanged predator turned and stared. He seemed to be wondering if he should eat me here or drag me back to the wife and kids. My eyes focused on his saber teeth while this giant cat sniffed the air and then roared. I slowly stepped back as shades of yellow ran down my spine. Retreating was one of the few skills I mastered in the military.

The AR-15 over my shoulder could destroy this creature, but I have always been a fan of big pussycats. To save this magnificent beast and me, my ultra-bright LED flashed on strobe and shined into his bright yellow eyes. My orange and black spotted friend did not appreciate the blinking glare of my one-eyed monster and exited stage left. After easing past where his tail slipped off the trail, my head kept turning back to see if my feline friend had changed his mind and wanted a taste.

Jungle shadows, squawks, and an assortment of rustling kept me moving at a steady pace. *Thank God for after-shave!* My cheap scent sent animals scurrying away in terror. Occasionally, something flashed across the path, but I only caught a fleeting glimpse. Voices inspired me to push through the side of this humid hole with arms wide. Worried that an attack was imminent, Dex greeted me with his lethal barrel pointed at my chest, and Stanley was holding a machete over his head. My entourage squealed with glee when they recognized me. I have that effect on people.

After introducing the team to my path, they were wary of a gloomy highway created by jungle critters. Given the choice to whack or follow, they reluctantly trailed behind and were delighted when we reached the clearing without meeting any varmints. The clean stairs immediately drew our scholars' attention while we, their stalwart guards, set up camp. Our professors, freed from their ivory towers, were ecstatic and climbed the pyramid taking close-up pictures of the Mayan glyphs carved on the front of each step.

As smoke curled up through the canopy like a handle-bar moustache, Dex shouted to the khaki ants clinging to the side of the pyramid, "Grubs on."

When the famished intelligentsia returned with their lips smacking, we forked into a concoction of beans and grease Dex called, "Camp Stew." Usually, I am a good forker, but this brown sludge had chunks of mystery meat that would challenge the hungriest connoisseur. My puckered lips spat them into the jungle to convince wild carnivores that we were not worth tasting.

During dinner, I shared my wit with our scholarly friends, but they ignored my attempts to prove I was not witless. As they lectured us in archeological lingo, my head nodded with a profound look on my face whenever it seemed appropriate. My suggestion for camp songs was vetoed without a vote. Bored by their ramblings, the predators surrounding us occasionally cried out that they, too, had heard enough of Mayan lore and pyramids. Jungle screams sent chills up and down my spine, but chills of any kind were welcome in this sweltering starless pit. Our enlightened archeologists passed their cameras around to let us marvel at the images carved on each step and, unfortunately, explained each one. After begging for ghost stories, their look of disdain shut me up.

Before surrendering to Morpheus and his dreams, it was my turn, "A guard with a gun should accompany you when nature calls. Eh! The jungle can surprise you even on the way to the latrine. Make sure you zip your tent closed after entering or exiting. Open tents invite jungle friends in to snuggle."

We headed to our tents when the fire turned to embers, and my head hit the sack with visions of marshmallows, chocolate, and graham crackers dancing in my brain. The two professors bedded down in separate tents on the other side of the fire from a tent built for two. Dex's mockery of edible stew caused the members of the Burwell Expedition to contribute to the jungle musk throughout the night.

✳✳✳

When morning beams filtered through the canopy, my body screamed for caffeine to get the sludge in my veins flowing. I crawled from the tent and rekindled the fire to heat a bitter brew. The first hot sip reminded me of a double-double from

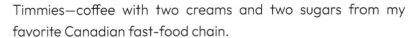
Timmies—coffee with two creams and two sugars from my favorite Canadian fast-food chain.

Dr. Livingstone eagerly cradled a steaming mug in his hands and renewed his aura when he swallowed my elixir. He walked to the steps to admire the hieroglyphics and pointed to a carving of Kukulkan. "He was an important god in the Mayan pantheon. He was depicted as a feathered serpent who descended from above to teach them the intricacies of life. I hope to determine if this pyramid was dedicated to him."

Still worried, my eyes searched for intruders, "I'm more concerned about the bare steps. Who kept them clean? Eh?"

The doc flipped his protective eyewear up on his slick pate before answering, "Didn't see any trace of people or villages on the way down yesterday."

"Yeah, but why aren't these steps covered with crap like the others?"

This wary academician threw up his hands and did not attempt an explanation.

Dex finally forsook his dreams and poured my aromatic concoction into a tin cup before he asked the professor, "What do you want to do today?"

After he slid his sunglasses from his bald dome to his craggy nose, this tedious scholar responded, "Our time is short. My academic proclivities tell me to concentrate on this pyramid."

Dex answered, "Fine, I'll guard you and Doc Anderson while Mick packs up."

We raised our voices to wake "Sleeping Beauty," but our chatter did not spur movement. I shook the tent frame and did my best imitation of Bugs Bunny, "What's up doc?"

After my clever repartee elicited no comment, I noticed the zipper on the tent was not pulled down and wondered if she was in trouble, "Cover up, I'm peeking in."

A doc-less tent greeted me. My expedition mates joined me in a cacophony of frantic shouts, but no lilting feminine voice answered our pleas. Livingstone volunteered to climb the pyramid, and Dex headed into the dark tunnel. I stayed behind to search the clearing for evidence of our missing Barbie or welcome her back. *An archaeologist should have enough sense not to gallivant around the jungle alone, but khaki is known to rot your brain.* Her cameras were gone. *She wouldn't take them to the toilet.*

Dex returned and shook his head in defeat. "No, blue-eyed blond in that green tunnel."

We shouted for the professor and added him to the list of missing archaeologists when he failed to answer our calls. Dex sighed and climbed the pyramid to find the bald one while mundane chores occupied my time.

Dex joined the list of missing persons when my desperate shouts were not answered. Dismay, concern, and worry furrowed my brow. What was going on? Eh! In Canada, if you go up, you must come down. My feet trudged up the steps with my finger on the trigger of my semi-automatic in case this was the part of the movie where Mr. "T" Rex, still hungry after devouring my companions, decided to chomp on me. At the top, my eyes checked the abandoned camp below. No professor with blond locks had returned to sample my morning brew.

Sweating buckets after a hot climb and searching for clues to the disappearance of my fellow explorers, my boot just missed crushing the professor's dark glasses. *At least he made it*

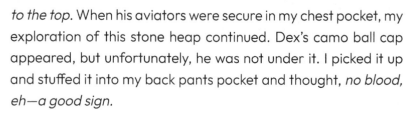

to the top. When his aviators were secure in my chest pocket, my exploration of this stone heap continued. Dex's camo ball cap appeared, but unfortunately, he was not under it. I picked it up and stuffed it into my back pants pocket and thought, *no blood, eh—a good sign.*

Scuffed leaves led me to a new set of steps, and my dull mind had a revelation, *Dex was dragging his feet to create a trail for me to follow.* Step by step, my feet silently mimicked his tracks down the staircase and then tiptoed through the jungle until voices sounded in front of me. The yellow streak down my back convinced me to leave the trail and belly crawl over the damp slime of the rotting jungle floor.

Peeking through the foliage at the edge of a small clearing, I discovered my friends were alive. Stanley and Dex sat on a log surrounded by a group of short natives in loincloths who were pointing spears at them. My debate over what to do ended when a spear pinned my head to the ground. A myriad of pricks in my back and butt made me understand the woes of a pin cushion. Dirty bare feet appeared before my eyes, and unwashed hands ripped off my rifle and pistol. Then a filthy foot literally kicked my ass—the universal signal to get moving. When this native entourage reached my buddies, I handed the professor his glasses and threw Dex his cap before sitting on the log next to them.

Dex caught his hat and complained, "Mick, you were supposed to rescue us. Nice job."

"I'm not the only one sitting on this log. Eh!"

A disturbance in the bushes made us look up. Someone was coming—probably El Supremo. I whispered a silent prayer and hoped he hated boiled food. Surprise, surprise! Pushing through the green wall surrounding us, our blond Goddess emerged with a toothy grin. Ulla stood before us and snapped a quick photo of the men assigned to protect her. "You guys are a sad lot. You're not going to believe what has happened."

She stepped closer and whispered, "These natives think I'm some sort of Mayan Queen. They bowed and took me to a small opening at the bottom of the pyramid. Professor, they let me come back to get you. You don't want to miss this."

My inquiring mind wanted to know, "You can talk to these guys?"

"With sign language. When they held up three fingers and pointed, I knew they were talking about my brave musketeers."

Ulla handed the professor her digital movie camera and whispered, "Film everything."

During our hike, I caught up with our savior and asked, "What happened."

She was eager to share. "I climbed the pyramid at daybreak to get pictures of the sunrise from the top when these natives surrounded me shaking spears. They kept pulling their hair and pointing at me. I stepped back, and a branch knocked off my hat. When my blond curls cascaded down, they fell to their knees in front of me and touched their heads to the ground. Not sure what to do, I raised my arms up in a sweeping motion above my head, and they jumped to their feet and smothered me. We had quite a celebration before they led me to the bottom of the pyramid and pulled out a stone block. They invited me to slide in, but you guys had to be a part of this."

***

The Burwell expedition turned on our flashlights, and the natives fired up their torches outside the not quite four-foot square opening at the bottom of the pyramid. The natives motioned for us to crawl in. *No way, guys. I didn't sign up to muck around under a pyramid. These khaki-covered fools can crawl into this snake pit without me.* But when Dex nodded toward the hole, I got on my back and squirmed in. This tunnel was tighter and longer than expected. Claustrophobia has never been a part of my repertoire of ills, but these walls started to pinch. About to panic, a chamber welcomed me and extinguished the desperate screams of panic forming in my throat.

After climbing to my feet, a vaulted ceiling formed an upside-down "V" only an inch or so above my head. *Ulla will have to leave her cowgirl hat behind.* The tunnel echoed when I shouted for company, and this pyramid swallowed the rest of the team like a hungry Mayan "Snake King." The torches and flashlights made the room glow after the others joined me. The archaeologists took pictures of the Mayan paintings on the walls that looked like they were brand new. These bright images were too high for our short companions to have painted unless, of course, they have invented step stools or ladders.

Ulla led us down a long dark stone block corridor with rows of Mayan symbols carved on the walls. Perusing the art and not paying attention, my foot tromped hers when she stopped and pointed at a weird green glow at the end of the hall. I apologized, but my demented mind could not resist a private thought, *the Burwell Expedition had just discovered the original light at the end of the tunnel.*

Ulla asked, "What's that?"

"Don't know but let me go first. That's what I'm here for."

At the end of the corridor, an unbelievable specter confronted us. There were three sarcophagooses, or is that sarcophageese? You know, the things the Egyptians used for coffins. These gray sarcophagi, wait, that doesn't sound right. Anyway, they were about seven feet long with black symbols carved on the tops. A thin band of green light escaped from under each lid and gave the dark cave an eerie glow. We approached these relics in awe. Ulla touched the first one and stopped to let the professor click a picture of her standing next to it. Dex headed for the second and carefully ran his fingers over the painted letters. My fingers ran along the gap of the third one where the ghostly green light leaked out and carefully lifted the lid. A bright green neon glow enveloped the room, and everyone looked at me like I had broken a Ming vase. Their frowns did not concern me. The spectacle before me made my body tingle.

There was no mummy. It . . . it was a small person, not quite five feet tall, lying on his back. Entombed in a long transparent tube with a square pillow tucked under his head, he was dressed in a loose-fitting white garment that resembled a judge's robe. He looked like a choir boy napping in a pew. This acolyte glowed green from the neon lights surrounding him.

Three square buttons outside the tube near his head had symbols that looked like Greek to me. The others nodded, and my undisciplined finger pushed the middle one down while everyone held their breath. The tube split and the sides slid into the base of the coffin. Satisfied with the result of the first button, my finger tapped the one on the left without consulting the others. Two hypodermic needles appeared from the sides of

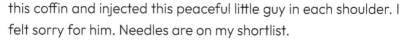
this coffin and injected this peaceful little guy in each shoulder. I felt sorry for him. Needles are on my shortlist.

Ulla pointed at the last button. One touch and an atomizer sprouted along this guy's neck and squirted a puff of yellow mist in front of his nose. We were surprised when the chest of this manly little man started to pump up and down.

Everyone got the idea and pressed buttons. The others were intent on opening these caskets until everyone stopped and stared at me. While I checked my zipper, Ulla raised her hand and pointed behind me. A glance over my shoulder found my little Mayan sitting up and staring at me. His skin was pale, and his bright smile revealed white teeth. His olive-shaped eyes blinked blue, and his hair reminded me of my yellow lab, but his nose was much shorter. His ears stuck out from under a short pageboy and were big enough to make me think of "Dumbo."

My new best friend placed one hand on the side of his coffin and held the other out to me. I was worried that touching him would infect me with an exotic disease but gambled and helped him down. Eyes opened wide as this unexpected guest shuffled to the next coffin and poked his finger into the side of his neighbor. Then he, no wait, then she climbed out without any assistance. Her feminine form made it quite clear she was not one of the boys. She had broad shoulders and was well over six feet tall. I wondered, *is this where "Amazons" got their name?* She had an oval face, and her hair was the same cut and shade as his, but her ears did not stick out. She had a short turned-up nose and looked like *Wonder Woman* in a choir robe with a Dolly Parton wig. Her grace and beauty immediately stole my heart. *Does dating a Mayan Princess come with a curse?*

These beings ignored us and strode with confidence to the first coffin. The lady inside hopped out on her own. She winked at me when her feet hit the ground. Obviously, Mayan women have great taste in men.

Twins? Wow! Ulla could be their sister. *Is Barbie an alien plant?*

The Mayan man took a hand-held device from his belt and touched the top. The bottom glowed red, and the sides flashed different colors. When all the sides were purple, he whispered into it and then returned it to his belt.

The professor was holding Ulla's video camera at his side and pointing it at the Mayans. I raised my eyebrows and nodded toward our new friends.

He whispered, "I'm getting it all."

Then these beings, Mayans or whatever the hell you want to call them, bowed to us, and it hit me. They reminded me of Japanese with blond hair and blue eyes. *Hum, Swedish Asians—a plethora of tangled ethnicity.*

The native guides bowed to these Mayans, and the members of the Burwell Expedition followed their lead, but these visitors from another world ignored us and looked down the tunnel and waved. We turned and saw a tribal leader with an elaborate feathered headdress marching two rows of Mayans down the hall. This new group looked like escapees from a Christmas pageant. Glowing headbands showered their white robes with brilliant light, and the tunnel glowed as they approached. They bowed to their friends and then to us.

Our Mayans returned to their coffins and grabbed clear circles. They switched them on and placed these glowing rings

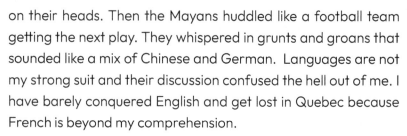
on their heads. Then the Mayans huddled like a football team getting the next play. They whispered in grunts and groans that sounded like a mix of Chinese and German. Languages are not my strong suit and their discussion confused the hell out of me. I have barely conquered English and get lost in Quebec because French is beyond my comprehension.

Without a word, they headed down the hall and left us behind. *Well, pardon me! How about a thank you? After all, we woke your friends up so they could call home.* I charged after them, and my fellow explorers jogged to keep up. Our procession looked like a line of Cardinals on the way to vespers at the Vatican.

Livingstone wheezed up beside me, "This is great. I'm getting everything."

Our parade turned down a new hallway that ended in stairs. We followed this choir up a spiral staircase that, after a long ascent, exited into daylight through an opening in the clearing I discovered at the top. More Mayans greeted our entourage, and we walked down the bare steps with lines of beings in flowing white robes in front and behind us.

This experience became even more astonishing when a real UFO appeared and wobbled as it lined up to enter the hole in the jungle canopy. This stainless-steel beauty was right out of Bed, Bath, and definitely Beyond. This miraculous spaceship was the size of a city block and had the classic dome on top of a saucer. A cloud-like mist formed fingers of white over the hull that looked like feathers. *Had Kukulkan returned?*

The natives dropped their spears, fell to their knees, and touched their heads to the ground. The Burwell Expedition looked up with our mouths agape trying to make sense of this . . . this incredible flying machine. Awe fought reality as my brain tried to comprehend the vision soaring overhead, and yet, I feared no evil. My mind searched for the truth, *are Mayans really aliens, or are aliens really Mayans?*

Static electricity made lightning crackle over the hull as this gleaming beauty descended. This alien vessel hovered over our heads and emitted the stink of sulfur that inspired the tales of hell drummed into me during the bible studies of my youth. The bottom was white, and two triangular black blades rotated in the center with lights on their edges. The glowing bulbs formed a perfect "Star of David" when they stopped spinning. *Was this the heavenly pillar of fire and cloud that guided Moses across the desert by day and provided light at night?*

Windows lined the craft above the rim, and Mayan glyphs were cut below. Two spinning circles surrounded the bottom—the outer one spun clockwise, and the inner one counter-clockwise. My thoughts turned to Ezekiel. He described his spaceship as a *wheel within a wheel.* Images of the Magi following the Star of Bethlehem crossed my mind. I would certainly pursue this starship with offerings of frankincense and myrrh.

The professor winked, "This will make us famous."

A brilliant stream of light shot out from under this majestic aerial phenomenon. A golden ramp descended to the ground and inspired thoughts of "Jacob's Ladder." I shook my head in disbelief as haloed men and women ascended the shining rungs into the belly of the beast.

Our original three extra-terrestrials bowed goodbye, but one of the twins took Doc Anderson's hand and motioned toward the light. Ulla pulled away and turned to Stanley, "You must come with me."

Ulla's winning smile made it hard for him to say no, but Livingstone was eager to join her. After a wink, he told her, "Let's explore the stars together."

The professor tossed me his camera and took her hand.

Envy was mine as they climbed the bright steps to their future. I would like to explore the universe. What a chance to learn of Mayans and men. Once they were inside, the ladder retracted, and the light flashed off. The whining of the spinning wheels turned to thunder. The Jewish star disappeared as the blades rotated and formed bright circles. My Argonaut's cap sailed into the wind as fire and brimstone blasted from between the wheels. This gleaming dragon left a smoking trail as it climbed into the blue. The jungle fauna waved goodbye as a cyclone of swirling gusts forced me to my knees. Once free of this earth, this visitor from another world hovered. My arms flew up, and my cry beseeched, "Behold, we on the firmament must contemplate the nature of heaven."

Then this object zipped from sight to unknown galaxies. The empty sky forced me to question what had happened.

Dex pointed at the camera, "Man, oh man, that was something! Eh! That video will make us tons of loonies."

"Proving extraterrestrials exist will be awesome. Eh!"

Dex told me, "Play it back. I need to see the video to believe what just happened."

I pressed the display button and touched the playback silhouette. No images appeared, so I tried again. The damn thing refused to reveal the treasures locked inside. Finally, I told him, "Nothing! It's blank."

Dex grabbed it and punched every button twice. Frustrated, he tossed it back and asked, "What the hell is wrong with that thing?"

After prying open the bottom, the problem was solved. Ulla and the professor may be great at digging up ancient artifacts but forgetting to insert a memory card questioned their understanding of modern technology.

Dex opined, "At least we have the coffins and stuff inside."

We turned to the pyramid and discovered that while we were entranced by the saucer, the natives had plugged the tunnel without any trace of the stone being moved. Our eyes searched for our indigenous friends, but they were gone.

Dex was worried. "No, docs! How do we explain that? We'll be snowshoeing into a blizzard when we get back."

"Easy Toto, we live in Oz. They'll believe anything in Ottawa. Just another bungle in the jungle. Eh!"

Tracy Biggar

Kitchener, Ontario - Canada

I enjoy writing about people who don't know how to define success.

4. The Smell of Success

Yes, the only way John could pass the exam was by cheating. Not easily done in a driving test. But this was the third time he'd tried, and he knew all the shortcuts, metaphorically and physically. For example, he made sure to schedule the exam on a day when snow was expected—the greater the snowfall the better. The examiner would take it easy on him, assuming he could drive expertly if he could drive at all in that weather. And John had lucked out. On the day his test was scheduled a blizzard was forecast. He worried the exam might be canceled, as he made his way into the test site through drifts waist high. Since the buses had been running so he presumed the DMV office would also be open. This was his last chance. He was supposed to start his new delivery job on Monday. Without a driver's license, it was not going to happen.

John's runners slipped and slid over the icy pavement as he made his way into the office. As his photo-grey lenses adjusted to the light he could make out very little. Yet where his eyes failed his sense of smell did not. His olfactory senses were assaulted with what could only be described as salamander stew doused in garlic paste and stirred with dirty feet.

"You aren't here for your drivers' exam, I hope," a voice from behind the counter caught his attention. John's eyes, now watering behind his photo-greys, turned towards a man holding a plate and gesturing at him with a spoon. "I didn't think you'd show up. I'm just getting some lunch here." Beside the man an ancient microwave, looking like it had been built for the space race, glowed and as he stood there some kind of glop dripped from the spoon onto his badly tied and sadly colored tie.

"Yeah, I'm here for my driving exam. I'm John Kitchen."

"Damn, hell, spit and bajeebers," The examiner's words entered the air accompanied by bits of smelly food. "You would show up today." The examiner sighed, as if reviewing his options. "All right then. I'll be with you in a minute." He turned to leave then turned back, "my name's Michael Benton by the way."

John smirked. The guy looked to be in his fifties. Of course, his name was Michael.

"You take a seat. I'll be right with you."

John did as he was told, smiling to himself that this Michael Benton fellow was already in the mindset to get this over with fast. "It's really coming down out there," he called out, though the examiner had disappeared into a back room with his plate.

John took off his parka and laid it over the chair beside him, along with his mitts and scarf, then stretched his legs out in front of him, and watched the puddles form around his wet shoes. The smell of whatever Michael Benton had been cooking still permeated the room, absorbed into the layers of dust on the plastic fichus, the stilled ceiling fan, the disconnected pay phone in the corner, and emanating back out. He remained alone, no one else was crazy enough to come out on a day like today, except for him – he knew the secret to the easy pass. Third time's a charm.

When Michael Benton finally emerged, he had dressed for the cold by adding red wool cap and yellow scarf and that was it, along with is already stained tie over his permanently wrinkled shirt. "Well, let's get 'er done."

"Don't you want to put on a jacket?" John asked, pulling his outdoor clothes back on.

"Nah. The car's got a heater."

"OK then." John followed Michael out the door into the blowing snow of the parking lot. The test car was buried under a foot of snow. Michael opened the back door to get the snow brush and a load of snow fell into the back seat, covering the upholstery. John reached in to give it a brush, but Michael stopped him. "Forget that. Nobody sits back there anyway." He handed John the brush. "Have a go. Let's see how you do prepping a car to drive in the snow."

John began meticulously removing snow and ice and flecks of any kind from the windshield, side windows, mirror, bumper, roof, hood, every exposed inch, though it seemed to land and begin to collect as fast as he removed it. Maybe a snowstorm had a disadvantage after all. He heard the car start up and knew that Michael was sitting in a waft of heat, blowing the smell of salamander stew, garlic and feet throughout the confines of the car. However, at least it meant that as the car warmed up, the snow evaporated as soon as it hit the windshield and hood. He was taking another pass at the roof when Michael rolled down the window and yelled at him to get in the car.

It was nicely toasty warm in the car, and a little ripe. John adjusted the seat, and mirrors, put on his seat belt, considered cracking a window but decided against it, and turned to Michael. "Where do you want me to go?"

"Head out of the lot and turn right."

"Got it." John moved the car ahead with what he hoped was the perfect mix of caution and determination. As he turned right onto Waterloo St. he eased the gas ahead, aware that the back wheels were already beginning to fishtail.

"Don't be afraid to give 'er," Michael advised, as he checked messages on his phone, not even looking up.

John sped up slowly and was beginning to close in on the maximum speed limit when Michael suddenly looked up and said, "Turn left here."

The car fishtailed again as Michael slammed on the brakes and turned the wheel. This guy was crazy! "Could you give me a bit more warning! I nearly did a doughnut there!"

"You're pretty young to be afraid of doing a doughnut. When I was your age, we'd head out to the Walmart parking lot after closing just to practice 'em. It's a useful skill to have."

"Am I being tested on doughnuts?" John asked, gripping the wheel.

"Not unless it comes up," Michael responded, vaguely.

As John was pondering this response the exit to the highway came into view. At least he was given some advance notice this time. "I want to you take the exit heading east."

"We're going onto the highway?"

"Do you have a problem with that?"

"I thought this test was for city driving?"

"Do you know how to drive on the highway?"

"Of course."

"Then it won't be a problem. You want your license you'll go where I tell you."

Everyone else had apparently gotten the memo that driving would be bad today, so they were the only ones on the road. At least John didn't have to worry about being rear ended as he frantically slowed at every drift. He passed exit after exit and had travelled probably twenty miles when he finally asked Michael where they were going.

"I just need to pick something up at my sister's in Fort Erie."

"We're going all the way to Fort Erie in a blizzard?"

"Sure. Do you have a problem driving in snow?"

"No. I guess not." John replied, then muttered, "But I didn't know I'd have to play UBER." Michael glanced over at him but apparently the sound of the windshield wipers frantically scraping snow from the glass had masked John's comment.

Finally, he began to see signs for the Fort Erie exit. He slowed and left the highway and followed the directions he was given to a completely snow-covered street on the south side of the city. John slowed the car and turned to Michael. "We will get stuck if I take the car in there."

"Well, let's see that you don't. Not getting stuck is kind of a deal breaker when driving in the winter."

John eased the car forward and could feel the tires resisting. He could feel Michael's suggestion forming on his lips so decided to make a pre-emptive strike and 'give 'er'. The car swept forward, slewing through the snow and at the large yellow house on the left with the snow-covered bikes scattered across the front lawn he turned into the driveway. Michael sat still, staring at his hands on the wheel.

"Well, turn 'er off. No use wasting the taxpayer's gas."

"I'd rather just wait here. You won't be long, will you?"

Michal reached over and turned off the ignition. "I have no idea how long I'll be. You got somewhere better to go?"

John was gearing up to tell him he had many better places to go, but Michael had gotten out of the car with the keys. Rather than freeze to death John opened the door and followed.

Michael's sister, wearing a ragged green velour robe and holding a Coors light in her hand met them at the door. "I never thought you'd show up in this storm."

"I couldn't put it off. I ate my last batch today."

"Well, get inside both of you. It's freezing out here."

John stepped in; screen door swinging in the wind in an attempt to close behind him, and pulled the front door shut over already forming drifts of snow. The hallway before him was lined with rows of not quite clean jars, stacked in wobbly towers and permeating over everything was the unmistakable smell of salamander stew, garlic paste and dirty feet.

"What do you mean you just ate your last batch? Did we come all the way over here, put my life in jeopardy for some of that . . . stew!" John bit back the descriptors he wanted to use. He didn't have his license yet.

"What are you complaining about? You passed, didn't you?"

"I did? Well . . ." John couldn't help the smile that spread across his face, short-lived as it turned out to be. Michael's sister took him by the arm and helped him navigate through the glassware lining the walls. "Congratulations. Hope you're hungry, I just heard on the radio that the highways have just been closed."

Tabitha F. Jenkins

Newark, New Jersey - United States

Tabitha F. Jenkins is a short story writer of fiction and poetry and was published in No Dear

5. In the Year 2019—Our Poodle and Dog Dixie Larry— Socket Was the Understudy

It was our Dog Dixie, sincerely the way father described him, was a scary cat of a white poodle. In the tub, where he shook and harlequined around in the water a Delmar Lazz, soaked Dixie, with Love, and the antiseptic soap. As a recognition of our success, in life's pandemonium, with the surname the Applegates, we all had cheeringly called him Dixie Larry Socket.

All of our heads turned and whenever we saw something to add, we stopped, "And then Dixie entered the room." This was out of not going into the sordidness that we knew you wanted to hear, the tangible secrets we never kept to ourselves, because we were the Applegates.

With the proximal extension of his dog appellation pet, name to represent Dixie, but in 2019 times were filled with a capitulation of needing that we had learnt from Dixie-what stirs the ability to have success as a family? Shouldn't it be the high mental wellness, of high people's cordiality and populaces, who suffer the most—and hospitably where the advent shock in the recollection of those high eviction notices couldn't go beyond the creationism of the one—everything was created by an omnipotent God—our family got last year.

I remind you, it stuck with the elastic tape, not skin tight or brick hard enough for a notice showed, the date we were supposed to leave, paper—secretion of nucleus on a microscope,

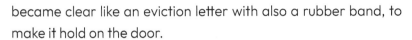

became clear like an eviction letter with also a rubber band, to make it hold on the door.

What it means to our family to practice in a run-down production in a closed down theater, we wrote the play, we made parts, we knew all the lines, and called it Marigold Hotel the seventies 1979 the Inn. And the kind of family with a picket fence, never been to one of those inns where the essence of the inn's ascent in meaning was Indian with zeitgeist 1940s Flare, religion, and theater.

One American family, one melting pot, where two Indian men chimed from 2:00 am in the morning wishing they could stay in America. Even though they were expected to take a plane back to India, the next day, there was a ruckus in the hotel Marigold of a pregnant lady, through the vents. They said she had an affair with the chef.

It seemed two female diners wondered when the husband would find out, as the picture of their marriage was dabbled with such lavish storytelling.

A while dining over hot flambeau, and fried French fries, they made it seem like this was the was the usual the chefs submissive with bowed heads, that leaping past their tall white hats with your eyes, anyone of them could of been the chef they were talking about who had an affair with the pregnant lady. French fries are so brown you thought the ingredients had been a little vanilla and a little chi.

The idealistic way to live, and thinking through the ear sockets when hearing about the affair, and the conversation so vexing we knew it was rush hour. According to the play's script there were two female diners considered married homemakers and dark-haired brunettes lived far from Hotel Marigold. During

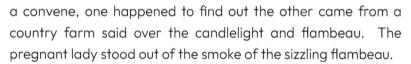
a convene, one happened to find out the other came from a country farm said over the candlelight and flambeau. The pregnant lady stood out of the smoke of the sizzling flambeau.

The chickens, homestead, and husbands who died replaced with a muscled twenty-something old farmer hand, they both recollected, in memory.

In the play The Inn at this conjecture one of the female diners was replaced with Dixie, Mom's turn in the play was cut short due to a quick casting change as in the Understudy for Mom was our Poodle. In this production of Marigold 1979 Mom played the original female diner.

We lived in Flatiron all our lives. It was amazing to see Dixie be Understudy for the first actor chosen. As we seemed as a family very tipsy and how we were sauntering around Flatiron after we got our first eviction notice, but from the retina of one's own eyes, all five of us became tipsy drinking Vodka, sans the highball glass you mix it in, and there was no Chardonnay left, in the bottle at the end of the day. Therefore, the five of us took a walk with Dixie the poodle and a silver lease through the streets of Manhattan.

This was when Donald Trump was President, when Melania Trump wore her I Really-Don't-Care-Shirt and when the Impeachment trials happened. Xander, was born in July, and he had been going through bouts of our Mom's acerbic cooking, of spinach, and floppy egg, cheese, on his high chair, and not being tipsy either. It was good too, Xander never became tipsy. The stories of Russian Collusion and Trump's Vladmir Putin in the days ahead were as turbulent as hearing about it from the car radio.

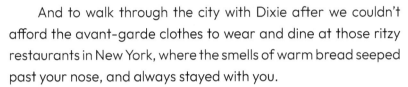
And to walk through the city with Dixie after we couldn't afford the avant-garde clothes to wear and dine at those ritzy restaurants in New York, where the smells of warm bread seeped past your nose, and always stayed with you.

We rehearsed the production Marigold Hotel the Inn, and everything changed after the first eviction notice as recognition of our failure, we were still the Applegates. I took a picture of Dixie, me Delmar Lazz Applegate, opposite the female diner lamenting about the affair. The Understudy took our Mom's place, the poodle Dixie Larry, at the dining table now in the cast of the play of The Inn, seated opposite the other female diner, this was the day and age when the first line of the play was "Who's the chef?"

Did you hear the pregnant lady had an affair with the chef? And was a substratum of her wandering around the hotel with runny lipstick on her mouth, and standing mendaciously on high platform, black leather boots—why Mendacious?

Because she looked, so muddled like shadow figures in erotica, or pornography they thought she lied to no uniform wearing cop/ sleuth, in Hotel Marigold - this accounting to where they were running to-and (they) referred to some of these hamlets dawned an apparent look of innocence, including the two men with the turbans—through this entailed as in the written thing we infer in the Play, they didn't just talk in the hotel all days, but out of coincidences like the two black haired homestead living, widows had been sitting down and eating a spoonful and seafood, in against the blaring flambeau that the two men with the turbans caught a whiff of this conversation.

A dozen patrons looked so quiet and calm, runny/ retina of their eyes, could be from food allergies, the chef's idea, and the ennui of a thought crept into his mind like lavender rise. And his eye, stitched to seeing everybody enjoy the vignette fish on a plate, the sight of a lost pregnant lady in those black platforms compounded by if she had bangs, fortitude. No are erroneous lies, in her saying the year was 1979, at the Inn, you couldn't see her, the pregnant lady because she didn't want you to, the wisp of a ghost with dark hair.

A disconsolate brunette although she looked sad in person, some of the people at the Hotel Marigold didn't come from where they said their origins actually were. And this (point) seemed to be the question-or lie prevaricating. when Dixie the Understudy—in the range of most outstanding lines, or a dark barking—to let out where did the pregnant lady go? According to this story the black-haired brunette lived on farms, as par, if the success of their lives didn't amount to the failures that the Applegates were soon to encounter.

If they were told to look at the helm of the chef's hat, to see the height of it, was it a representation of success—over prevaricating with a lie? Some who stayed at the Inn (as in the hamlets at Hotel Marigold) weren't being veracious (honest) about where they came? Some weren't sure about the Applegates, how could they get an eviction notice, if Xander the newborn, would be the emblematic sign of success.

Ethan Ellisor

Wimberley, Texas - United States

A beginning writer in college as an English Major hoping
to work in the game idustry.

6. The Hunter and the Wolf

Deep in the dense woodlands of the north, there was a village. an unknown little dot on only the most thorough of maps. The ground only yielded the thinnest stalks of wheat, the sparsest of berries, and skittish animals. It's a miracle the town was founded in the first place, but its people found happiness in the struggle. Everyone worked to procure their share, shoring each other's homes up against the cold, gathering herbs to treat sickness, to make the most of the hostile land.

But there was a man who went above and beyond the town's virtues to help his fellows. The man was an expert huntsman, one whose unparalleled hunts and plentiful bounty made him the village's savior in its harshest months. Dedicated to his work, the Hunter was always careful to never overhunt, setting out for days at a time to vary which herds were preyed upon. With all his care to keep the prey plentiful, it was quite the strange find when one of his hunts found all his fields and traps empty. Confused, the Hunter quietly made his way from place to place, each as empty of prey as the last. Poor hunting was common in Winter, but this utter absence was far more ominous to the Hunter. Finally, just as he was beginning to think he was the only life in those woods, he found a trail. A long, crimson smear, bright against the freshly fallen snow. Carefully and slowly, The Hunter followed the bloody trail, the woods ahead filled with distant howls and faint cracks and tearing sounds.

It wasn't long till he arrived at the edge of a clearing, the shadowed mouth of a cave hosting the source of the sounds he'd heard. Ashen grey wolves, prowling along the mouth of the hollow was an immense pack of them, sharing a king's feast of veal and hare between themselves. At the head of this excessive banqueting was a truly monstrous wolf whose dark fur seemed to devour the snow that fell upon it. The only color marring the perfect black was the blood of the elk it dug into. As the Hunter watched this beast—the cruel light of intelligence and hunger he could see in its eyes told him all he needed to know. This was a traveling pack of wolves, a sort who needn't care at all for maintaining the herds like he does. He was certain these came from the same cut of cloth as the worst of human hunters, driven by prizes and limitless want rather than just need.

In the dead of winter, a pack like that could spell doom for the Hunter and his village, scraping by as they already were. Yet to try attacking a wolf pack directly would only end with his body added to the feast. With a clear strategy, the next day he prepared his traps, weaving ropes into snares, simple traps to scare and harry the pack to urge them to seek new hunting grounds. He felt hope as he spied one get caught, its leg going into a snare, but in moments that beastly black wolf appeared, shearing the rope in a clean bite. This surely felt like an act to mock the Hunter—it spent the day digging through the snow to uproot the rest of the traps.

Frustrated at two days wasted away without even a scrap of prey to catch, the Hunter returned home to gather harsher traps. Steel jaws, cruel perhaps to lay down such things, but some cruelty was worthwhile to the Hunter if it meant evading a slow and hungry death. Though however well concealed the traps were, that forsaken Black monster never failed to evade them. It's taunting bounds going right over or right around. The Hunter spent the day watching, checking each trap, but all were empty of predator or prey, without a drop of blood. However, the Hunter was a focused man, even if it meant putting aside hunting for a time, the pack's greed was too dangerous to leave alone.

Day after day, the Hunter tested every facet of his skills in trapping, using all the tools at his disposal, more steel jaws, net traps, sharpened spikes of wood. In an act of desperation, the Hunter even took some of his own dwindling food and poisoned it, but all too clever as usual that damned leader of the pack refused to touch those cuts of meat. Time wore on, and the Hunter's stomach could tell, growling louder and louder in his ears. His escapades and inability to hunt had left both him and the village with half-empty stomachs. He knew they wanted answers, and more than answers food, so after another grueling day of taunting evasions by the pack, the Hunter turned from frustration to earnest rage.

The Hunter, ill-rested and hungry, found himself kept up at night and plotting. He had one more plan, a rash plan many would say, but undeniably deadly. One that would be enough to rid the village of the monsters. With a triumphant clap of his hands, the Hunter rode through town, collecting lantern oil from every villager who would grant it to him, promising they'd be glad they gave it over. With a bounty of oil gathered in a few jugs he set out with an excited vigor known only to those who believe themselves close to a great accomplishment, or in the greatest depths of delirium. While the monster's pack was out on one of their hunts, the Hunter wasted no time dousing the cave with oil, adding kindling and dry grasses across the ground. All that was left was to wait, sitting as still as a statue the Hunter waited with a morbid excitement as the first wolves returned.

He counted meticulously, and once each and every ashy coat believed itself safe, the Hunter watched as the black coat returned and smiled. With a few strikes of flint, he ignited a rag-covered arrow. In a single smooth draw of his bow, the hunter brought the burning arrow all the way back, the dancing flames starting to singe his frost-bitten fingers. The streak of flame launched in a perfect arc into the dark maw of the winding cave.

The result was instantaneous, the quiet winter air suddenly filled with the bloodcurdling howls and yips of pain of the pack. The flaming pack burst forth from the glowing mouth of that cave and darted madly into the forest, trying desperately to flee the inferno, some failing to even escape that roaring maw. Of course, the last to climb out of that kiln of rage was the black wolf, walking without panic, not fleeing. As the Hunter stepped out from his cover to get a better look at his great foe, he saw that the cruel light he'd seen behind its eyes now looked saddened. The beast staring right into the Hunter with a sympathetic, almost pitying look. The beast did not run as the fire burnt its coat to ash. It simply stared as it died.

The Hunter, exhausted as he was, could not help but let out a loud victorious shout, forgetting his hunger and weariness in the face of his own vicious joy and the dancing fires in the cave. Fueled by this, the Hunter stumbled through the woods, eager to return home, eager to rejoice with the townsfolk for their rescued supply of food. The Hunter was far too caught up in his revelry to note the heat upon his back. But to his confusion, he was not met with accolades and praise, no instead his neighbors stared at him questioningly, horror etched onto their faces. Perplexed he tried to explain, telling them of the wolves he had been hunting, telling them that they would soon be eating well once again. But as the cold response of his peers slowly sobered him, he finally noticed the heat conquering the frigid air.

Slowly, now filled with the same horror he'd seen in his fellow villagers, the Hunter slowly turned to look behind him. Even with bleary, sleep deprived eyes he could see the dark forest lighting ablaze, flames licking high into the cloudy sky and devouring that snowy ancient forest. The Hunter had indeed rid the town of the wolves, but only to fulfill their role himself. Realizing what he'd done as the first sparks start to fly toward the village, the Hunter screamed for everyone to pack what they own, to gather the horses and flee. There was little to motivate the villagers to stay, but the Hunter did everything he could, gathering the horses and helping people carry what they needed. But as the Hunter tried to join a wagon leaving, he found himself shoved to the ground. No one wished for him to follow in whatever new life he'd doomed them to, rightfully so he thought. Now as the Hunter lay there, watching the horses ride off, he wondered if it would be the flames or the cold—they left behind that would kill him.

Jeremiah Mack

Washington, District of Columbia - United States

I'm a junior at SUNY Oswego, NY with the ambition of pursuing a career as a comic-book writer.

7. I was Running

Before I got out of bed, I rested my earphones in a charger. I touched the Bluetooth setting on my laptop and disconnected my earphones so I could connect them later to my phone. I checked the time on my phone—8:17 pm. I thought, "I can make it-for sure."

Still wearing my pajamas, I got out of bed to open two drawers under it. As the wood and metal scraped against each other, the grinding sounds they produced were annoyingly tolerable. I grabbed my goto cherry Marvel T—shirt from one, and a pair of sweatpants from the other.

FLIT, FLIT. FLAP. I heard fluttering sounds behind me. I looked back—it was my roommate, asleep. He tossed and turned in bed and pulled the blanket up to cover his shirtless mid—back. The room was dark, except for the opened blinds that let the streetlights' glow that shone in through the window. The whooshed sound both of our fans made added some soothing noises to our room.

I took off my nightshirt to put on my Marvel shirt. My sweatpants were on the bed. I stared at them and looked back at my sleeping roommate.

"I don't have time to change in the bathroom," I thought. I grabbed the pants and hid behind the two stacked dresser drawers in our bedroom. They provided some cover to do what I did. I frantically slipped off my pajama pants and hurried to put on my sweatpants.

"Ugh." I groaned when one leg refused to come off smoothly. I yanked it off. Rustling from the bedsheets. I looked up. Still asleep. I prayed that he wouldn't sporadically get up out of bed and see my skinny naked body. I flipped the pajama over my shoulder and quickly lifted the sweatpants over my legs and waist.

I checked my phone—8:20 pm. I was running late, but I felt like I could still make it in time—I just had to.

I clicked on the ceiling light and opened my closet halfway. I quietly grabbed my hooded jacket off the hanger. It still made a sound. CLANG. *Sorry, Roommate.* I also grabbed another jacket and threw it on top of my hoodie. I slipped my shoes on and tied them. I laid my phone and earphone case in my secure jacket pocket. I looked in the mirror and placed on my mask—I adjusted it so it wouldn't look crooked. I put my winter hat on. I made sure to adjust it as well. Low enough to cover my forehead but not my eyebrows.

I opened the door and my right foot almost landed on the carpet floor. I almost forgot something—my keycard. I scurried to my bookbag and grabbed my card and placed it in my pocket. I was finally off.

I clicked the elevator button. DING. I hopped on and pressed the first floor. I grabbed my phone and my earphone case, 8:22 pm. I connected my Bluetooth to it and put the one working earphone in. *Yes, I can make it.*

DING DONG. I left my res hall. I speed-walked to the campus center. My normal walking pace.

I didn't know why I walked so fast. I remembered a while back—I was at a Walmart with my friend two years ago. I pushed the cart that had our groceries. When we entered the store, I

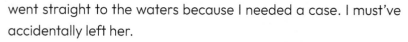

went straight to the waters because I needed a case. I must've accidentally left her.

"Jeremiah!" She screamed my name.

I turned around and saw her jogging at me.

"Why are you walking so fast?" she painted.

"I was? This is how I usually walk."

I cut through the campus center because it was the fastest route to my destination. Much quicker than walking around the way I used to do. I exited on the other side. The wind almost blew me to the ground. *Good thing I didn't wear a cap.* I played the first opening, "The Hero" of *One Punch Man* on a loop. Every time the second chorus came on, I turned up the volume and tried to mouth the lyrics.

8:24 pm. I raced down a street. It was pretty dark, with no street lights shining as I walked. I clicked on my flashlight to not step on anything "dirty." I turned it off when I crossed the street. Other people were walking in the same direction I was headed. That made me walk even faster. I scurried past most of them.

8:26 pm. I ran past the building's sign, "Lakeside Dining Hall."

I finally made it to my location—Lake Night Dining. I arrived at the doors, and there it was, my nightmare. A line of hungry people. The line extended outside, in the freezing wind. I failed my mission.

CHATTER, CHATTER. The others. I grabbed my spot before they arrived. They witnessed the same horror.

"Hell no," one chuckled as she walked back.

I saw people inside the hall also walking back when they peeked and saw the line. I looked at my phone—8:28 pm. Two minutes before they opened the doors. Well, it was more than two minutes for me since I waited for several others to move the line.

"Next time," I thought, "I'll leave around 8:12 pm. There shouldn't be a long line by then." *Right?*

Nicole Hwang

Brookline, Massachusetts - United States

8. Kindness

An ant was trekking through the forest looking for his colony. He wasn't quite sure when he got lost—the colony had all been carrying food and water back home, and he veered off path to take a quick break. By the time he woke up, the rest of the line was gone! But it wasn't *his* fault they got lost; they could have just waited for him to wake up. He was the colony's baby— what would they do without him? They must be so worried.

The ant crawled under chartreuse patches of moss and teetered over large logs. At one point, he swam through a pond and left pinpoint-sized footprints on the dry leaves of the forest floor. (What a shame that he was too small to hear them crunch!). Yet, there was no sign of the colony, and he was beginning to feel frustrated.

The ant walked onto a path of woodchips, where he saw a wild dog sleeping next to a great tree stump. Ah! Finally, someone who could help! His six tiny legs raced over to the furry creature. He called out to the beast, "Dog, have you seen my colony?"

The dog snored.

Undeterred, the ant climbed onto the dog's rough, hairy paw and jumped up and down. He climbed onto her back, stomping all the way into her nostril. Upon crawling in, he scaled along the walls of her nose, scratched, and kicked. Just when the ant was about to make his way towards the dog's ear, she sneezed violently and the ant went *flying* out of her nose.

"Oh, finally! Dog, you're awake. Have you seen my colony?"

Groggy, the dog looked at the ant and sized him up, however you can size up a 3-millimeter-long animal. . . then she breathed out deeply and rolled her eyes. The ant stood oblivious to the dog's snark, maybe because ants don't have good vision or maybe because he just wasn't paying attention.

"Can't a dog get her beauty sleep these days?"

The ant continued speaking. "Can't you help me? I don't know where my family went."

". . .Why do you think I would do that."

The ant stared. Why *not?* "Because I need help. . .?"

Who even are you? To disturb my quiet time like this. . ." the dog tsked. "I've spent enough time talking to you. Please leave and let me get my rest."

But the ant didn't leave; in fact, he sat in front of the disturbed dog and waited. The dog closed her eyes to go back to sleep. . . and opened them again after a minute. Was the ant still there?

He was. And ignoring the dog's grumbles, he climbed into her back.

As the ant rode on the dog's back, he kept pestering her with demands. "Can we go slower? I can't see." Oh, how the dog wished she could just shake him off!!

***

At one point during their trek, the dog came across a raging river. She crossed shakily, placing careful paws on the algae-dressed rocks and slipping with every step. Meanwhile, the ant snored away, nestled on her back.

***

After hours of searching, the ant saw a familiar log. He jumped up from the dog's back; the wind blew him into the air, and his legs wriggled as he fell onto a rock and rolled down. He tumbled down joyfully as the dog watched him descend.

The colony rushed forward and enveloped the ant. The dog waited for him to turn back, to give her some kind of reward or thanks or acknowledgment for bringing him back, but he was rushed inside without a word. Not one look was given to the great, hairy, kind beast. She stood outside in the blowing wind, with nothing left to do but turn around and go back to her tree stump.

E.A. Garone

Long Neck , Delaware, United States

Dr. Eugene Garone, a published writer, enjoys writing
fiction about unusual events and situations.

9. Misfitted

"Please state your name."

"My name is Arnold Hale."

"Arnold Hale!" The Chancellor repeated. "Do you, Mr. Arnold Hale, understand why you have been arrested?"

"No, sir. I am not quite sure."

"You are not quite sure," he repeated in a cynical voice.

"And you do not know why you have been called to appear before this jury?"

"No, sir, I am truly not aware of it."

The twelve jurors of the tribunal sat motionless.

"The reason why you are here should be clear enough by now."

"I am sorry, sir. It is not clear. I don't quite understand."

The tyrannical Chancellor took a deep breath.

"Then first, let me ask you a question."

"Yes, sir, you can ask me anything you want."

"What is your occupation, Mr. Hale?"

"Well, sir, I am writer."

"Well, sir, he is a writer," the Chancellor said mocking his captive's voice.

The tribunal sat motionless.

"And what exactly is the kind of writing you do, Mr. Hale?"

"I write poetry, sir."

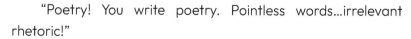
"Poetry! You write poetry. Pointless words...irrelevant rhetoric!"

The tribunal sat motionless.

"And what do you write about, Mr. Hale?"

"I write poetry about how beautiful God made the world... the landscapes...a morning sunrise...pretty flowers...life...and death."

The authoritarian interrupted...

"Well let me remind you that according to government law, God no longer exists."

"You say that God no longer exists, but how can all the beauty in the nature be proven?"

"Well, let me remind you that the government states that nature is only the outcome of evolutionary blunders, Mr. Scribbler of useless words!"

"You say that I write only scribbles, but words allow us to see, hear, taste, touch, and smell everything in the world."

"A ha! So, you think you can see, hear, taste, touch, and smell words, Mr. Hale? That is absurd!"

The tribunal sat motionless.

"It is not absurd, sir. I use words for creative expression."

"Nonsense!" The Chancellor folded his hands in front of him. "Let me remind you that we no longer have the right to express ourselves through creative writing. Useless words will only weaken our society."

"But sir, words cannot weaken society...people do...words are powerful."

"Ridiculous....words do not have power...the government has power!"

The tribunal sat motionless.

"Sir, before the insurrection, haven't you ever read a poem that made you cry?"

"Crying is foolish and useless," one of the members of the tribunal blurted.

"Those who cry are weak and unfit for society," shouted another."

"But to cry shows that we show emotion, and that we are human!" Arnold refuted.

Chancellor shrieked so loudly into the microphone on the podium that it squeaked.

"Crying shows weakness! And there is no tolerance for any emotion in our society!" he yelped.

"But sir...sometimes reading a poem can bring tears to my eyes."

"Poetry brings tears to your eyes because you are a weak little man who believes in God and reads weak worthless words."

"Words are not worthless, sir," Arnold hesitated. "Are you saying that words written by poets such as Edgar Allan Poe? Walt Whitman? Sylvia Plath? Langston Hughes? or Maya Angelou are worthless?"

The chancellor's face reddened. "Inconsequential!"

The tribunal sat motionless.

"Their poetry is all literary propaganda...emotional trash... rubbish!" he shouted.

"But poetry is not rubbish, sir."

"Yes, indeed...poetry is rubbish. Artificial Intelligence controlled by the government tells us what to read and does all the writing now. Therefore, there is no longer a need for irrelevant words written by a misfitted man such as you."

The tribunal sat motionless.

Arnold lowered his head.

"My words are not irrelevant, sir!"

The tribunal gasped waiting for the Chancellor to attack. The dark, cavernous room became silent. Then the Chancellor spoke.

"Now do you understand why you have been arrested Mr. Hale?"

"Yes, I do understand now, sir."

The Chancellor shouted "Yes, it is because you are weak and misfitted for society!

He hesitated. "And are you aware of what can happen to those who are weak, misfitted writers who put their own useless emotions before government law and logic?"

"I am not quite sure, sir."

"Well, let me tell you what will happen, Mr. Hale. The twelve members of the tribunal will huddle together to cast their votes and if you are found guilty, you will be sent to a government facility to undergo reprogramming."

Arnold though for a moment, then asked, "If I am reprogrammed, then I would never be able to feel any emotion or write poetry again?"

"Precisely!" The Chancellor shrieked slamming his fit on the podium.

Arnold paused for a moment then looked up at the Chancellor and began to speak. "If that is so, then may I have one last request, sir?"

"A last request?...May I have a request, sir?" he said ridiculing Arnold. "How dare you ask such a pathetic question."

The tribunal gasped.

"I would like to recite a poem to you and to the tribunal."

"He wants to recite a poem. He is not only a weak, misfitted writer, but a fool!" the Chancellor said turning toward the tribunal. "Shall I grant his request?"

The twelve tribunal jurors leaned forward and nodded.

"Well, well, Mr. Hale...the Chancellor paused. "I will make one exception and grant you your last request before the jury decides on your fate. I will do it only because I want to make an example out of you and show the rest of society how misfitted writers are."

The tribunal stirred.

"Guards! Unshackle him!" he ordered. The chains clanged as they freed the offender from the chains. Arnold stood up at one end of a table. Six tribunal jurors were standing on one side of him, six on the other. The Chancellor sat perched in the middle on his podium.

The room was so quiet that a low din of white noise filled the air. The poet took a deep breath and was ready to begin.

"Ahem." Arnold cleared his throat and then he spoke. His voice echoed in the cavernous room, reciting each line of his poem with clarity, determination, and passion.

"Who will be there to mourn?
When alabaster feathers float
and whispering summer breezes
turn to frozen winter snow.

Who will be there to mourn?
When reverence and compassion
brings forgiveness, truth,
and meaning to my life.

Who will be there to mourn?
To sleep in endless rest
with a protector at my side
healing my troubled soul.

Who will be there to mourn?
Will life have any meaning or
forgotten over time?"

Arnold looked up and spoke softly through the stillness.

"Who will mourn for you, Chancellor, when you die?"

An eerie hush silenced he room. Arnold watched as his accuser trembled trying to hold back tears. Then the Chancellor began to speak in a soft, quivering voice.

"Mr. Arnold Hale," he said as his water-filled eyes reddened. A teardrop glistened as it rolled down his face. "I do not know who will be there to mourn for me when I die."

The twelve stoic tribunal jurors no longer sat motionless. They saw the Chancellor's emotional reaction to Arnold's poem and huddled together.

One of the jurors began to speak turning toward the person sitting at the microphone. "Weakness in our society is forbidden. And you have exhibited weakness, Chancellor. Therefore, the tribunal has determined that you are the guilty one here today, not Arnold Hale!"

The Chancellor yelled "NO!" as the microphone squealed.

Then the tribunal began chanting in a macabre-like dance, spiraling closer and closer to their doomed leader. Eerie ohm-like sounds echoed in the sterile room as they surrounded the Chancellor. They lifted him up in the air, six on one side, six on the other as he kicked, yelled, and shrieked in anguish. But they ignored him.

"No doubt you are more of a misfitted man than a poet could ever be," Arnold said as he watched the twelve member of the tribunal carry the Chancellor out of the room to undergo reprogramming.

Our Anthologies

- Unforgettable
- Just A Minute
- One Night Stand
- It Was A Mistake
- Swinging Through Childhood
- Revenge
- Historic Tales
- Phobia
- Business Stories
- Just Another Minute
- Love Is In The Air
- Three Words
- Wanderers Heart Recluse
- Collecting Memories
- Blue Collar
- Students Hustle
- Mythology
- 7 Deadly Sins
- Just One More Minute
- This Was A Mistake
- Games and Sports
- When There Is A Will There Is A Way - Motivational and Inspirational Stories
- Fairy Tales
- Vernacular
- End Of Days & Wars
- Night Clubs
- Stories Relating To The Environment
- Score A Word Prompt Volume 1: Word Prompts For Those Love To Write
- Road Trip To El Dorado
- Zeitgeist Hellacious Sharent Money Nomophobia
- Christmas and Halloween
- Speaking Of Romance
- Wishing Well
- Dialogue At The Bar With Drinking Partner
- What A Mistake
- Door Bell
- e-Leading Arrogant Lives
- Snake Pit
- Political Power Play
- Business Stories Startups and More
- In Flight
- Hitting The Dead End
- Been There Done That
- Adding Just A Minute
- Xylem Justice Is Served
- Honestly Speaking Dishonestly

Printed in the USA
CPSIA information can be obtained
at www.ICGtesting.com
JSHW010239261023
50895JS00006B/24